NI

BIBLICAL TRUTHS

CONCERNING
DIVORCE & REMARRIAGE

ISBN 978-0-9976944-0-6
Published by Better Life Group

Design by: TJ Flow Designs
www.tjflow.com

www.nikiwinston.org

CREDIT WHERE IT'S DUE

I would like to dedicate this work to Pastor Daryl Barnett. Without you, sir, I would not have been able to even begin this research. You are a gift to the body of Christ and marriages everywhere, and I credit the overarching message of this work to you. Thank you.

CONTENTS

iii

ACKNOWLEDGEMENT

I always want to acknowledge my husband, David S. Winston. I couldn't ask for a better man with whom I can walk out God's purpose and share my life. You are, and always will be, my favorite person!

1 BACKGROUND

My Personal Story

When I met my wonderful husband, I was a divorcee with two beautiful boys. Without going into great detail, I will say that my first marriage was very rough. I entered into it at 19 years old, thinking I was marrying a man of God, and over four years later I was a shell of a woman with two children to care for. I genuinely felt like I was rescued from that marriage (by God) and countless experiences have confirmed to me that I did the right thing by ending it. About four more years passed and I met David – a truly wonderful person and a man who seeks to love me as Christ loves the Church. What is even more important is that we both agreed early on that our relationship was to glorify God and raise the standard for godly relationships. As stated in our "Relationship Mission Statement" (which we created four months into the relationship), the number one reason we wanted to be married was to "be a more powerful force for the Kingdom of God!" Time after time our relationship has been confirmed and affirmed, by God, by others, and by the fruit it has produced. That's why when I was confronted with this issue, head on, I had a problem with it. Something wasn't right. I NEEDED to do further study.

The Confrontation

Several years into my marriage to David, I felt God leading me to teach women, single and married, how to be better wives. For an entire year, I had monthly meetings with a group of ladies (all ages), teaching from and further developing a curriculum that I had created. Much of this was from the difficult lessons I learned while striving to be my best in my first marriage, but more was from the grace and revelation that God had given me to be a great wife to David.

I credit my husband's unwavering positive confession that he's spoken over me since the beginning, always referring to me as an AMAZING wife, and giving me the space to grow without scorn or judgement. His pure love is powerful, and it has freed me to be able to receive revelation from God on this topic. At the end of a year, God led me again: This time to write the book, *How to Win Him and Keep Him Happy: Secrets to Becoming an Amazing Wife*. A website, some social media outlets, and speaking engagements were, of course, to follow, but what was of significance to *this particular* research was a video I posted online about "Healing and Remarriage." For the next detail, it's important to mention that I am a minister, and everything I am mentioning here is from a Christian perspective.

The public may comment on most YouTube videos and since mine focused on the healing I received from the Lord, mine were getting a lot of comments from the Christian community. Most were very positive and appreciative, but two comments in particular were of concern. One very "helpful" person laid out for me, in detail, the only ways in which I was allowed to be divorced or remarried, and let me know that if my marriage did not fall into one of these categories, I was essentially committing adultery with my husband. Another cut straight to the point and told me I was going to hell. Of course I dismissed the latter because they obviously did not have a revelation of the saving and sanctifying grace of God. That "If we confess our sins, he is faithful and just to forgive us our sins and to cleanse us from ALL unrighteousness."[1] The former, however, was the catalyst to my research.

I can no longer find their comment, but they quoted one of the synoptic gospels, which, as it pertains to my research, are all very similar. "But I say to you that everyone who divorces his wife, except on the ground of sexual immorality, makes her commit adultery, and whoever marries a

---

[1] 1 John 1:9 (English Standard Version).

5

divorced woman commits adultery."[2] Whoa. Now I had remembered skimming this in the past, and perhaps even consciously saying to myself, "Well, it's covered in the blood. I've repented for any wrongdoing in my previous marriage and situation." But now I was a marriage author, and presenting myself as an authority on the topic. While qualified to teach what I was teaching, and possessing special revelation for marriage and wifehood, I STILL needed an answer for this, because no-doubt it would come up again. This accusation against me was just a catalyst to search deeper.

But my heart didn't convict me. I was so sure that I was in the center of God's will in my marriage and that I was exactly where I needed to be in life's journey – my destiny, which

---

[2] Matthew 5:32 (English Standard Version).

INCLUDED my husband – that **I knew there was no way that God would have me in a situation that was causing myself or my husband to perpetually commit adultery!** This, I believe, is where your faith and your intimacy with God is tested. When you have an intimate relationship with God and know His nature, you will differentiate from His voice and someone else's. "My sheep listen to my voice; I know them, and they follow me. But they will never follow a stranger; in fact, they will run away from him because they do not recognize a stranger's voice."[3] I "ran away" from the input of this stranger (as opposed to running away from God, thinking He's condemning me), because I know the character of my God so well. I know Him as a loving and merciful God, and He would never trick

---

[3] John 10:27 (English Standard Version).

me or lead me astray. **I read these words about divorce in my Bible, but I couldn't connect them with my wonderful, merciful Lord, so I decided to seek more information.** And what I found out was very interesting…

Seeking Help

Because I believe in honoring your elders and their wisdom, I first went to the highly revered, Pastor Daryl Barnett, that used to serve as a Pastor in our church. His revelation on marriage may be unmatched. It is known that he dedicates much of his study time on this topic, and he is widely respected on the matter. I messaged him, explaining my quandary, and he responded with, "Sure I can help, just give me a call. You're in the clear!" I was glad to hear that, and that my instincts were correct. During the call, he explained some things about translation, God's will for His people, and how ministers never seem to want to study this issue out entirely, by going back to the original Greek and Hebrew for answers. This laid the foundation for my research and motivated me to study more, and when I got the chance to research this for a paper, I jumped on it!

2 THE COMMON ARGUMENT

Currently, most English versions of the Bible translate the few verses we find concerning the dissolution of marriage in the New Testament similarly. Texts on this topic are found in Matthew, Mark, Luke, and 1 Corinthians – Not in John. Matthew and John are the only two of the gospel writers who were part of the first twelve disciples, and therefore the only two that would have been present when Jesus was speaking on the matter. Based on these facts, and because there is nothing concerning this in John, we will be treating only the text found in Matthew. In the interest of brevity, I will not be addressing 1 Corinthians, but I invite you to take an additional look at it after reading my research, as well as Mark 10:2-12 (which only adds a sentence about the disciples asking Jesus about what He said), Luke 16:18, and Matthew 5:31-32 at your leisure, and you will find that everything I show you here lines up with these scriptures as well, including any original Greek translation. We will first take a look at the scripture (Matt. 19:3-9) in the most common English translation as this is the starting point from which I will assume most of us are familiar.

> And Pharisees came up to him and tested him by asking, "Is it lawful to divorce one's wife for any cause?" 4 He answered, "Have you not

read that he who created them from the beginning made them male and female, ⁵ and said, 'Therefore a man shall leave his father and his mother and hold fast to his wife, and the two shall become one flesh'? So they are no longer two but one flesh. What therefore God has joined together, let not man separate." ⁷ They said to him, "Why then did Moses command one to give a certificate of divorce and to send her away?"⁸ He said to them, "Because of your hardness of heart Moses allowed you to divorce your wives, but from the beginning it was not so. ⁹ And I say to you: whoever divorces his wife, except for sexual immorality, and marries another, commits adultery.⁴

Wow. This is a lot, right? And if we read the English Bible as-is, and interpret it literally, with no underlying meaning or context, then it seems as if divorce may be prohibited by Jesus, and that if one DOES divorce and remarry, they are guilty of the

---

⁴ Matthew 19:3-9 (English Standard Version).

sin of adultery. This would mean the people who told me I'm committing adultery would be correct. Now, I want to take a moment to say that this research isn't just for me. I am confident enough in God's mercy and grace to know that I would be covered no matter what, but **people need an answer and a proper interpretation of God's Word on this topic of divorce, and who better to give it to them than a Christian marriage teacher?** In addition, I feel compelled by the Holy Spirit, and have been encouraged by my husband to teach on this. We will take a closer look at translation in the next section to find the truths in this scripture.

Before going into translation, I'd like to bring up the question of "good reasons for divorce." Some might say, well what about a case of extreme abuse? What if a woman were tricked into marrying an abuser, he beats her regularly, threatening her life (and at times seeming to almost take it), beating her children, and endangering the family in general? One would most likely say, "Well, of course she should leave! She should take the kids and get out of there! And if he shows no signs of restoration, she would be justified in divorcing him. As a matter of fact, this would probably be safest." Then as the story goes, a knight in shining armor comes along, sweeps the whole family up, and everyone is loved, taken care of, and lives happily ever after, right? Most would be in agreement with this conclusion, but if we take the scripture literally, she and her new husband are in the perpetual sin of adultery. That hardly seems fair – and it hardly seems like Jesus. That's because it's not.

3 PROPER TRANSLATION, BACKGROUND AND INTERPRETATION

When studying the Bible, we must give way to proper translation (or lower/textual criticism), **the background** (or context and setting) **in which something is stated, and proper interpretation** or understanding – or, more simply put, the heart behind which the statements were made – **the "why."** One incorrectly translated word in a sentence can change its whole meaning, sending God's people down a false doctrinal path.

The same goes for context. For example, 1 Corinthians, as we know, was a letter written *to* the Corinthian church. If readers didn't recognize this, and weren't familiar with "…the chaos and lack of order rampant in that assembly," they would think that Paul was saying no women should speak in ANY church.[5,6] Obviously, this is not the case. Paul was addressing a very specific issue, and even mentions women prophesying and filling leadership roles in the church in other parts of the New Testament, *including* 1 Corinthians. In addition to translation and context, **it helps tremendously to have an understanding of God, and know Him intimately – to truly understand His Word. And**

---

[5] Gotquestions.org. "Do women have to remain silent in church?" Gotquestions.org. January 27, 2017. Accessed October 12, 2017. https://www.gotquestions.org/women-silent-church.html.

[6] 1 Corinthians 14 (English Standard Version).

interestingly, He has set it up so that the more we study His Word, the more we know Him and will understand it. It's a beautiful cycle. Studying God's Word will grow your intimacy with Him, help you know His heart, and ultimately increase your power and effectiveness for His Kingdom.

THE DIFFERENCE BETWEEN "DIVORCE" & "CERTIFICATE OF DIVORCE"

Divorce: "Divorce" and "Certificate of Divorce" are not the same thing. Every time you see the word "divorce" in the New Testament, it is the same word in the original Greek. Actually derived from two words, *apo* and *luó*. *Apo* is defined as "from" or "away from," while *luó* is "loose, untie, release, destroy."[7] Collectively they could

---

[7] Bible Lexicon. Accessed October, 2017.

have several similar meanings, such as: "set free," "release from," or "putting off" of the wife.[8] This conjunction of words was used many times in the Bible, also meaning "to send away," such as when Joseph found out Mary was pregnant. The literal translation was that he was going to "send her away."[9,10] It also translates to "let go," "loose from," "let go free," and more. **In fact, this term is indicative of a regular practice of Jewish men, historically and at that time, of literally *walking out on* their wives, and even families.**

---

http://biblehub.com/lexicon/. Taken from the NAS Exhaustive Concordance

[8] Barnett, Daryl, Pastor. "Conversation on Biblical Divorce and Remarriage." Telephone interview by author. March 23, 2017

[9] Matthew 1:19 (New American Standard Bible).

[10] Bible Lexicon.

Sometimes the men would just leave, and sometimes they would send the wife away, but **this term is not implying ANY type of official divorce.**

The Jewish Law actually corroborates this translation. In Jewish Law, if the husband wants to dissolve a marriage, he "…must consent to give his wife a bill of divorce ('get'). If he refuses, the wife remains locked in a non-existence marriage, unable to remarry. There are hundreds, possibly thousands of women trapped in this situation in Israel and throughout the Jewish world."[11] Hoffman sums up this law, mentioning that "…a husband was able to take a second wife without leaving the first one…"[12] This refusal to officially divorce was

---

[11] Chetty, Denzil. *Divorce Discourses: A Biblical Dilemma.* New Delhi: Concept Pub. Co., 2007, x.

[12] Hoffman, Joel M., Dr. *The Bible Doesn't Say*

common, even in modern times, and does in fact, separate the concepts of an *official* divorce and simply *leaving* the wife/marriage. **Although the Jewish Law reflects the "certificate of divorce" referenced in Matthew, which was also a reference from the Mosaic law, there is a second option, so to speak, of "putting off" the wife by simply walking away from the marriage: Two separate things.**

Certificate of Divorce: After the Pharisees asked Jesus if it was lawful for a man to "send away/put away/walk away from" his wife, they asked Him another question. "Why then did Moses command one to give a certificate of

_____

That: 40 Biblical Mistranslations, Misconceptions, and Other Misunderstandings. New York, NY: St. Martin's Press, 2016, 203.

divorce and to send her away?"[13] This term for "divorce," whenever it is coupled with "certificate," anywhere in the Bible, is not the same word as "divorce" by itself. "Certificate" here in Greek is the word *biblos,* meaning "book" or "roll,"[14] probably best thought of like a scroll in that day – an official document. "Divorce," here, is the Greek word *aphistémi,* which translates, "to lead away" or "depart from."[15] **So "certificate of divorce" here could best be defined as an "official document of departure," and does actually mean (official) divorce as we know it.** Thus verse seven could also be translated as "Why then did Moses command one to give [an official document of

---

[13] Matthew 19:7 (English Standard Version).

[14] Bible Lexicon.

[15] Ibid.

departure] and to send her away [or *apoluó*: release/walk away from her] ?"

Once again, it is clearly seen that these are two separate concepts – by the fact that the Pharisees (and the original Mosaic Law) separated them in the previous sentence. The Greek word used here for "send her away" was the SAME word that English translators decided to use for divorce. Perhaps it was more convenient, but research into history, culture and translation all point to this being incorrect. **The English word here is wrong, thus our understanding of this passage is wrong. We must read with a new translation in mind.**

Even Jesus didn't treat these two concepts equally. Jesus said everything on purpose, and they were JUST talking about (official) divorce before that. If He MEANT divorce, why wouldn't he have expressly said it? Why would He change the verbiage to mean something else? Because they are not the same. *We* must also differentiate between the two, because they are both Jewish realities. **What we are seeing is not just in this passage. It is the same EVERY SINGLE TIME you see these two words in the entire Bible, including the Old Testament!**

The Same in the Old Testament?

Jesus was referring to the Mosaic Law found in Deuteronomy 24 when responding to the Pharisees. Let's look at this.

> When a man takes a wife and marries her, if then she finds no favor in his eyes because he has found some indecency in her, and he writes her a certificate of divorce and puts it in her hand and sends her out of his house, and she departs out of his house, ² and if she goes

and becomes another man's wife, [3] and the latter man hates her and writes her a certificate of divorce and puts it in her hand and sends her out of his house, or if the latter man dies, who took her to be his wife, [4] then her former husband, who sent her away, may not take her again to be his wife, after she has been defiled, for that is an abomination before the LORD. And you shall not bring sin upon the land that the LORD your God is giving you for an inheritance.[16]

Here, in the Hebrew, "certificate" (*sepher*) is also translated as a "document" or "book" (official document), and "divorce" (*keritut*) is "to cut off/cut down."[17] So we can safely say that it is an official document, cutting ties (or covenant), just like the "official document of departure" we found in the New Testament. He then says to put it in her

---

[16] Deuteronomy 24:1-4 (English Standard Version).

[17] Bible Lexicon.

24

possession, and to send her away (from *shalach*).[18] **This *sending away* is the same concept that we find in the New Testament Greek (*apoluó*), once** again, differentiating these two, even in the Old Testament. ***First make it official, THEN send her away.***

Even Malachi, translated using the word "divorce," is consistent with this methodology. Let's look at what one scholar found when searching Malachi for answers on the topic:

> "…the text does not say: 'I hate divorce'. The closest he can come to generating a confusing English translation for the confused Hebrew is 'For [or: 'if'; or 'when'; or 'indeed'] he hated [or possibly: 'hating'], send away! [or possibly 'to send away']'. 13 The same confusion is found in the Greek translations, and the Latin Vulgate for 2:16 is cum odio habueris dimitte

---

[18] Ibid.

('when [or: since] you hate [her], send [her] away'."[19]

Once again, the Hebrew word here for "divorce" has the same root *(shalach)* as in Deuteronomy, meaning "to send," and lines up with the Greek translations we are also finding in *every* instance in the New Testament.[20]

---

[19] Moloney, Francis J. 2015. A new testament hermeneutic for divorce and remarriage in the catholic tradition. *Australasian Catholic Record, the 92* (3): 269-288, 273.

[20] Bible Lexicon.

4 WHY DOES IT MATTER?

The Law and Adultery

So why does this all matter? What does the difference in translation prove? It begins to unveil the motivation behind what Jesus is saying in the gospels. Let's start by going back to the Mosaic Law. When God told Moses to permit divorce, yes, He was doing it "because of the hardness of their hearts" (which we will soon enough address), but He made His statement in a very specific way, as

God always does.[21] The certificate of divorce was not referring to the sending away of the wife (*apoluó/shalach*), as this was not part of the law itself. **This portion of law was referring to the fact that a man MUST give his wife an official document, breaking covenant, BEFORE he could send her away.** Why?

Lightbulb! THIS IS IT!!

If a man walks away from or sends his wife away WITHOUT giving her an official document of release (certificate of divorce), cutting ties/covenant with her, then *she is still married!* If she, in fact, DOES remarry without getting that release of covenant from her first husband, what is she doing? Committing adultery – and HE has caused her to do it!

---

[21] Matthew 19:8 (English Standard Version).

This is what is meant when Jesus says, "And I say to you: whoever [walks away from] his wife, except for sexual immorality, and marries another, commits adultery."[22]

If inside the marriage covenant one commits adultery then, according to biblical standards, they have already broken covenant. If the husband were to walk away from his wife at this point, and to marry another, he would not be breaking covenant with his first wife by way of adultery, because the covenant had already been broken. If they were married and no one had yet broken covenant (by way of adultery), and he decides to walk away from her and remarry (or vice versa) WITHOUT an official document of departure/cutting covenant ties (certificate of divorce), then they would still both be married (and

---

[22] Matthew 19:9 (English Standard Version).

29

under covenant). In this instance, a subsequent marriage by either would be considered adultery. This leaves us with the conclusion that **if they were married, but the husband presented her with an official document of departure/cutting covenant ties, then she would no longer be married, thus not committing adultery in a subsequent marriage**. This seems almost too simple to be accurate, but I will present you with an example straight from the book of Judges.

Example

> But Samson was furious about what had happened, and he went back home to live with his father and mother. [20] So his wife was given in marriage to [his companion] the man who had been Samson's best man at the wedding. Later on, during the wheat harvest, Samson took a young goat as a present to his wife. He said, "I'm going into my wife's room to sleep with her," but her father wouldn't let him in. "I truly thought you must hate her,"

her father explained, "so I gave her in marriage to your best man.[23]

In Judges 14, Samson found a woman and married her. After a situation made him angry (verses 19-20), we see that Samson left her without word and went to his father's house. Then her father gave her in marriage to one of his companions. This is a precise example of the "putting off" or more vividly demonstrated, "walking away from" a wife that is being referred to all throughout scripture. It's such a perfect example, in fact, that the story even goes on to demonstrate how this would cause her to commit adultery. In Judges 15:1 (the very next verse), Samson comes back to visit "his wife" (note the scripture continued to refer to her as his wife even

---

[23] Judges 14:19b-15:2a (New Living Translation).

though she was now married to another), saying "'I will go in to my wife in her room.' But her father did not let him enter."[24] This language further proved that Samson felt still married because going "in to" her implies sexual intimacy.

So what are we seeing here? **We see that Samson walked out on his wife without an explanation, and clearly without any official covenant breaking document.** In this case, Samson did not intend to divorce his wife, but we can deduce from the situation that this scenario was common, as her father not only married his daughter off in Samson's absence, but he spoke in "divorce language" when he told Samson (best demonstrated by the NASB) "I really thought that you hated her intensely; so I gave her to your

---

companion."[25] This "hated her intensely" is more precisely, but less eloquently translated "hate (like an enemy)," *plus* "hate (like an enemy)." So it's like a double version of hating someone to the point of being in complete opposition to them. **The result was that Samson's wife committed adultery against him by marrying another without an official document of divorce from Samson.**

A New Translation

So for the sake of the most applicable translation, and in light of Samson's example, let's use the term "walk away from" to replace the word "divorce" from here in the scripture, and "official document, cutting covenant ties" in place of "certificate of divorce." We will now redefine

---

Matthew 19:3-9, then look at what else is there to further dissect.

> And Pharisees came up to him and tested him by asking, **"Is it lawful to [walk away from] one's wife for any cause?"** 4 He answered, "Have you not read that he who created them from the beginning made them male and female, 5 and said, 'Therefore a man shall leave his father and his mother and hold fast to his wife, and the two shall become one flesh'? So they are no longer two but one flesh. What therefore God has joined together, let not man separate." 7 They said to him, **"Why then did Moses command one to give a[n official document, cutting covenant ties] and to send her away?"** 8 He said to them, "Because of your hardness of heart Moses allowed you to [walk away from] your wives, but from the beginning it was not so. 9 **And I say to you: whoever [walks away from] his wife [without the benefit of an official document of departure], except**

for sexual immorality, and marries
another, commits adultery.[26]

So things are getting clearer. **We see that
Jesus is NOT saying that remarriage after an
official divorce is adultery. He is instead
responding to the culture of the time by saying
that when a man *walks out on* His wife
(without the benefit of an official covenant-
cutting document), the next marriage is
considered adultery (because the first marriage
covenant still exists).** But there still remains the
question: Did Jesus just make a law against divorce?

---

[26] Matthew 19:3-9 (New American Standard Bible),
emphasis added.

5 DID JESUS CREATE A LAW AGAINST DIVORCE?

Let's look at Malachi again: "Malachi 2:10-16 criticises Jerusalem and Judah for their unfaithfulness to God by paralleling their behaviour with husbands unfaithful to their wives...the text does not say: 'I hate divorce'."[27] As we saw earlier, God hates when one walks away

---

[27] Moloney, 273.

from another. In addition, many argue that this scripture isn't even about two humans.

> "Later Christian interpreters and rabbinic thought have turned to Malachi 2:16 for biblical support for the absolute prohibition of divorce. But this is a misuse of the original text (which remains confused), and would not have influenced Jesus of Nazareth in any way. When Jesus comes to discuss divorce, he turns to the Torah texts of Deuteronomy and Genesis. He never mentions Malachi."[28]

If Malachi were about marital divorce, and Jesus was trying to prohibit divorce, He very likely would have included it in His discourse.

Dr. Joel M. Hoffman agrees that the translation is off, calling the Hebrew in Mal. 2:16 "odd" and says it "borders on ungrammatical," but after analysis decides that even if the

---

[28] Ibid.

"modern translations of Malachi 2:16 are right, the line is still not about divorce in general. **Like other prophets, Malachi was comparing God's relationship with Israel to a marriage.** Two verses earlier, Malachi says that 'the Lord was a witness between you and the wife of your youth, to whom you have been faithless, though she is your companion and your wife by covenant.' **Malachi's point is that Israel (as represented by Judah) has abandoned God's path. In this context, 'I hate divorce' makes the most sense as a statement about 'the divorce we are talking about, [Israel and God]' not [marital] divorce in general.**"[29]

He goes on to say, "So the Old Testament does not condemn divorce, though in singling out divorcees, it reflects the emotional impact of divorce."[30] I think it is important to note here that

---

[29] Hoffman, 204-205.

[30] Ibid., 205

there is no law in the Old Testament prohibiting divorce. We see in Deuteronomy that the laws are *governing* divorce, which is clearly legal (for men to women only), and in Malachi, neither the translation nor the context allow for a prohibition of divorce. **This means that if Jesus were to be prohibiting divorce, He would be creating a new law.**

The idea of creating new laws seems out of character for Jesus. He said He came to fulfill The Law. As a matter of fact, in that same passage of scripture, He goes on to say that "…until heaven and earth pass away, not an iota, not a dot, will pass from the Law until all is accomplished."[31] The words "iota" and "dot" in this verse are literally the smallest letter in the Hebrew alphabet and an apostrophe. Jesus was not

---

[31] Matthew 5:18 (New International Version).

trying to change the rules. He seemed very interested in keeping the Law as it was, then fulfilling it. When asked by the Pharisees for the greatest commandment in the Law, Jesus (being God and required to tell the truth) could have said anything, but instead of coming up with some awesome *new* revelation, He quoted *The Law* (Deut. 6:5), and said "You shall love the Lord your God with all your heart and with all your soul and with all your mind."[32]

The Law was of utmost importance to the Jewish people. Trying to change a law from one that details the proper way to dissolve a family to instead disallowing the dissolution of said family would have been unacceptable. One of the reasons Jesus came was to set a new standard of conduct,

---

[32] Matthew 22:37 (English Standard Version).

but He did not come to create new laws. It is not reasonable to think this was Jesus' intent, but let's investigate further to be sure.

MORE TRANSLATION

The two elements of this portion of scripture we need to examine are "What therefore God has joined together, let not man separate," and the last part of "Because of your hardness of heart Moses allowed you to [walk away from] your wives, but from the beginning it was not so."[33]

"Let Not Man Separate"

It is easy to look at the common English translations of "…let not man separate" and assume it means "we will not let man separate" or more clearly stated, "man is not allowed to

---

separate," however in spirit, this verse doesn't seem to mean this.[34] I went in search for the translation of the word "let" in this verse, and *found* that the word "let" is not to be found here in the original Greek![35] It seems this English word "let" has been added for eloquence and flow. The original Greek roughly translates "that which God unites together, not [human] man separate (or divide)." This implies more of an inability than a directive, for example "cannot," or probably more accurately "does not." So more accurately translated, not for flow or eloquence (eliminating the existence of "let"), this verse would say "that which God unites together, (human) man does not divide."

---

[34] Matthew 19:6 (English Standard Version).

[35] Bible Lexicon.

If we are honest with ourselves, this sounds more like Jesus. A good example of this style of communication is when He showed the disciples how to pray in Matthew 6. "Our Father in heaven, hallowed be your name. Your kingdom come, your will be done, on earth as it is in heaven."[36] This passage is a good representation of the simple, direct language that Jesus often speaks in. He states His prayer as if it IS. He doesn't say "*Let* Your Kingdom come" or "*Let* your will be done..." In the original text, the word "let" was neither in the statement about man dividing what God unties, nor is it in this passage. Adding it here would be similar to how they added it into verse 6 in Matthew 19, changing its meaning. This is simply a difference in the opinion of the translators

---

[36] Matthew 6:9-10 (English Standard Version).

between two verses, adding it to one and not the other. **So this verse is not Jesus disallowing us or "not letting us" do something. It's not a prohibition, and is definitely not a new law. It's Jesus stating the obvious: "You (man) don't have the ability to divide what our Creator has united."** The question we really need to be asking is "What has God united?"

The Big "But"

Verse 8 ends with "...but from the beginning it was not so."[37] Again, one of the words here is added for flow, but if used for interpretation implies a rebuttal: the word "but."[38] It helps flow, and is justifiable to keep, but (just like the "but" that came before this parenthesis) it seems to

---

[37] Matthew 19:8b (English Standard Version).

[38] Bible Lexicon.

negate or deny the statement before it. This would sound like "I just said that Moses let you do this because of your hardness of hearts, but I don't agree with it and I'm about to tell you why it's wrong/unacceptable." If we take out the "but" and go with original Greek language, this translates more like, "For your hardness of heart, Moses (turned to) permitted you to walk away from your wives. It was not this way at the beginning."[39] Jesus calls it "…an accommodation to the Pharisees' hardheartedness…" but it wasn't "…God's original intention at the Creation."[40] **He was undoubtedly admitting that the Mosaic Law was not the best way, but it was permissible. He was**

---

[39] Matthew 19:8 (English Standard Version).

[40] Gundry, Robert H. *A Survey of the New Testament, 5th Edition.* Grand Rapids: Zondervan, 2012, 170.

saying that God's perfect will was for them to stay together.

"Genesis 1:27 and 2:24 describe the situation between a man (Adam) and a woman (Eve) before the introduction of sin into the human story (see Gen 3:1-24)."[41] God intended from the beginning for man and woman to be together forever – but then, sin. Enter hardness of hearts, and an earthly provision for this. Jesus came to undo (or forgive us) the consequences of sin, and of course His perfect will – just as is God's – is for it to "be on Earth as it is in Heaven" like it was in Eden.[42] But this being God's perfect will and the prayer of Jesus, doesn't make it a command in the way that many have postured it. It is God's

---

[41] Maloney, 285

[42] Matthew 6:10 (English Standard Version).

desire, just like it's His desire that we should all live in peace with one another.[43] **The fact that this portion of scripture is paired with mistranslation and misinterpretation about the sin of adultery has caused readers to misinterpret it, changing its original meaning and significance.**

An Even Newer Translation!

Now that we have an even more thorough re-translation of this passage of scripture, let's lay it out one more time, replacing all of the phrases we've discussed, and see now how it reads.

And Pharisees came up to him and tested him by asking, **"Is it lawful to [walk away from] one's wife for any cause?"** 4 He answered, "Have you not read that he who

---

[43] Romans 12:18 (New International Version).

created them from the beginning made them male and female, [5] and said, 'Therefore a man shall leave his father and his mother and hold fast to his wife, and the two shall become one flesh'? So they are no longer two but one flesh. **[Man doesn't have the ability to divide what our Creator has united.]**" [7] They said to him, **"Why then did Moses command one to give a[n official document, cutting covenant ties] and to send her away?"** [8] He said to them, **["For your hardness of heart, Moses permitted you to [walk away from] your wives. It was not this way at the beginning.] And I say to you: whoever [walks away from] his wife [without the benefit of an official document of departure (cutting covenant ties)], except for sexual immorality, and marries another, commits adultery.** [44]

---

[44] Matthew 19:3-9 (New American Standard Bible), emphasis added.

IT'S ALL ABOUT THE COVENANT

So what is Jesus really trying to get through to us here? Marriage is important, and so is sexual purity, but why is Jesus so adamant specifically about adultery and not also abuse or even some other important marital issues? Because **Jesus is not simply after the marital sin of adultery here, but its *significance!* Although this is a detail about marriage not to be taken lightly, it is meant to serve as a metaphor for our covenant with God.** Marriage, throughout the Bible, is a symbol – THE symbol – of our covenant with God. We are the bride of Christ in the New Testament, and throughout the Old Testament marriage is repeatedly used by prophets to symbolize the relationship between God and His people (and unfortunately also their faithlessness, or apostasy).[45] We are God's spouse. Adultery is breaking covenant with one's spouse. Whoever says they are God's, making a covenant with Him, and worships another god, is committing adultery against Him, breaking covenant. While His, they are making covenant with another. **In the passage above, broken down into the examples above,** *each one lays out how to avoid covenant-breaking adultery.* **"Jesus is after the covenant."**[46]

---

[45] Revelation 19:7, Ephesians 5:23, Jeremiah 31:32, Isaiah 54:5 (English Standard Version).

[46] Barnett

6 CONCLUSION

Divorce between two spouses is not officially prohibited anywhere in the Bible, nor does the Bible actually say that God hates it. But God loves His children so much and surely hates the pain that divorce causes for them. In addition, He doesn't want any of us (spouses or children) to have to experience being walked out on with no word and no closure. One of the most painful things that can happen to someone is to be abandoned or rejected. Adultery is only committed against someone if you are still in covenant with them. With an official decree of divorce (as opposed to just walking out on someone with no agreement), the two spouses have broken covenant and are free to remarry. **God's original intent is for a marriage to stay together, and the Word encourages us to grow into great spouses, but nowhere does it imprison God's people whom He loves in a painful, miserable, or dangerous marriage.** People are too important to God, and He doesn't want them hurting, as is reflected in Jesus' ministry. What's most important to Him are the people (not the marriage vow itself), and the covenant they have with HIM.

Is divorce a sin? At the VERY least, on the side of one spouse, I absolutely believe sin is there.

Divorce is difficult, painful and no doubt surrounded by sin. Whether one person sinned enough for the both until the situation was unbearable or even dangerous for one (making the act of divorce equal to an escape, sometimes from a life threatening situation), or it was both parties committing the many sins of neglect and selfishness until one or both decided to break the covenant they made with one another; in divorce, most would agree that sin doth abound. But where sin increases, grace increases all the more, and where there was a broken person, assaulted and damaged by the ravages of sin, God's grace is powerful to heal, restore and grow that person into someone who can be a gift and a light for His Kingdom and even Kingdom marriages everywhere![47]

---

[47] Romans 5:20 (English Standard Version).

7 WHAT ABOUT THE WOMEN?

Addendum: Addressing the Apparent Gender Inequality in these Scriptures

Why doesn't Deuteronomy address the women in the same way it addresses men? In the verses above (Deut. 24:1-4) The Law is only addressing men concerning divorcing the women, and does not give instruction to women about divorcing men. In Luke 16:18, Jesus is also speaking only to men, as well as in Mark, *when speaking to the Pharisees*. But when the disciples privately asked Him about walking away from a wife in the book of Mark, Jesus spoke in a way that was gender-equal, saying, "Whoever [walks away from] his wife and marries another commits adultery against her, and if she [walks away from] her husband and marries another, she commits adultery." (Mk. 10:11-12, ESV, emphasis added) Matthew's version also leaves out the gender equality.

The simple explanation for Deuteronomy and even when addressing the (Jewish) Pharisees is that **there was no need to address women who wanted to divorce their husbands. It was illegal in this culture.**

> "The normal Jewish view according to rabbinic law, was that a man could be said to commit adultery against another married man,

and a wife could be held to commit adultery against her husband, but a husband could not be held to commit adultery against his wife. According to Jewish Law, only the man had the right to divorce his wife… [and] a wife had no right to divorce her husband." (Chetty, 112)

Since [Jewish] women could not divorce their husband when this was addressed, there would be no need to address that issue – because it never happened. In fact, **it would be strange, and could have ruined Jesus' credibility with the Pharisees if he had publicly addressed women divorcing, because it would have displayed a lack of respect for the Law.** Another thing to note is that Matthew was written for a Jewish audience, so **if there were contradictions to rabbinic tradition or law, he (Matthew) may have left those out in order not to taint the gospel's witness to the Jews.**

But in Mark, when speaking to His disciples, privately, Jesus addressed men and women equally, regardless of Jewish customs (Mk.10:12). The book of Mark was addressed to Romans, and therefore could (and should) more loosely reflect their laws. Jesus put men and women on the same level in order to include the Roman law, which "...gave the woman her right to divorce her husband." (Chetty, 112.) Rome wasn't all the way progressive, however. There were still double standards in their culture. For example, "...women could not cite adultery when filing for divorce because society viewed it as a given that married men could have sexual relations with mistresses, prostitutes, and slaves without fear of social stigma or recrimination." (Nardo, 63) "Women were often subject to such double standards in marital matters." (Nardo, 64) The act of divorce itself wasn't one of these double standards. In Ancient Rome "…more liberal social attitudes and the enhanced social position of women had made divorce more common. Both women and men could now initiate it…" As a matter of fact, for Romans, the social stigma of divorce was so minimal at this point that "…no reasons for the breakup had to be given." (Nardo, 62)

Jesus' diversion from Jewish tradition could also be reflecting the overarching theme of the New Testament concerning equality in Christ, regardless of race, gender or social standing (free or slave, rich or poor). It is likely in this instance, however, that the more modern culture of Jesus' day, in contrast to Moses' was the cause for this.

To summarize, **concerning gender equality, as a Jew, Jesus diverted from the norm. He, just like in almost every other area,** was a pioneer for equal rights: for women, race, and social status. In most cases, when we notice what seems like unfairness or inequality on the part of Jesus, we can often trace it back to a reason of cultural sensitivity, or even just a case of Him knowing how to best affect His audience. Neither Jesus nor the Bible forbid modern women to divorce on the grounds that they are female.

Bibliography

Barnett, Daryl, Pastor. "Conversation on Biblical Divorce and Remarriage." Telephone interview by author. March 23, 2017

Bible Lexicon. Accessed October, 2017. http://biblehub.com/lexicon/. Taken from the NAS Exhaustive Concordance

Chetty, Denzil. *Divorce Discourses: A Biblical Dilemma.* New Delhi: Concept Pub. Co., 2007.

Gotquestions.org. "Do women have to remain silent in church?" Gotquestions.org. January 27, 2017. Accessed October 12, 2017. https://www.gotquestions.org/women-silent-church.html.

Hoffman, Joel M., Dr. *The Bible Doesn't Say That: 40 Biblical Mistranslations, Misconceptions, and Other Misunderstandings*. New York, NY: St. Martin's Press, 2016.

Knust, Jennifer Wright. *Unprotected Texts: The Bible's Surprising Contradictions About Sex and Desire.* New York: HarperOne, 2012

Moloney, Francis J. 2015. A new testament hermeneutic for divorce and remarriage in the catholic tradition. *Australasian Catholic Record, the* 92 (3): 269-288.

Nardo, Don. *Women of Ancient Rome.* San Diego, CA: Gale Group, 2003.

Gundry, Robert H. *A Survey of the New Testament, 5th Edition.* Grand Rapids: Zondervan, 2012

10613587R00038

Printed in Great Britain
by Amazon